NECESSARY NUTRIENTS

Carbohydrates as Necessary Nutrients

BY AMY C. REA

Kids Core
An Imprint of Abdo Publishing
abdobooks.com

abdobooks.com

Published by Abdo Publishing, a division of ABDO, PO Box 398166, Minneapolis, Minnesota 55439. Copyright © 2023 by Abdo Consulting Group, Inc. International copyrights reserved in all countries. No part of this book may be reproduced in any form without written permission from the publisher. Kids Core™ is a trademark and logo of Abdo Publishing.

Printed in the United States of America, North Mankato, Minnesota.
102022
012023

THIS BOOK CONTAINS
RECYCLED MATERIALS

Cover Photo: Shutterstock Images
Interior Photos: iStockphoto, 4–5, 6, 12, 14; Marilyn Barbone/Shutterstock Images, 8; Shutterstock Images, 10–11, 20, 28 (top); Alena Kos/Shutterstock Images, 16; Robert Kneschke/Shutterstock Images, 18–19; Prostock Studio/Shutterstock Images, 21; Red Line Editorial/Shutterstock Images, 23; Alex Katkov/Shutterstock Images, 25; Jeny Che/Shutterstock Images, 26; Brent Hofacker/Shutterstock Images, 28 (bottom); I. and S. Walker/Shutterstock Images, 29 (top); Bartosz Luczak/Shutterstock Images, 29 (bottom)

Editor: Ann Schwab
Series Designer: Layna Darling

Library of Congress Control Number: 2022940683

Publisher's Cataloging-in-Publication Data

Names: Rea, Amy C., author.
Title: Carbohydrates as necessary nutrients / by Amy C. Rea
Description: Minneapolis, Minnesota: Abdo Publishing, 2023 | Series: Necessary nutrients | Includes online resources and index.
Identifiers: ISBN 9781098290016 (lib. bdg.) | ISBN 9781098275211 (ebook)
Subjects: LCSH: Carbohydrates--Juvenile literature. | Carbohydrates in the body--Juvenile literature. | Carbohydrates in human nutrition--Juvenile literature. | Nutrition--Health aspects--Juvenile literature.
Classification: DDC 613.2--dc23

CONTENTS

CHAPTER 1
What Are Carbohydrates? 4

CHAPTER 2
Why the Body Needs Carbs 10

CHAPTER 3
Best Choices for Carbs 18

Nutrient Jobs 28
Glossary 30
Online Resources 31
Learn More 31
Index 32
About the Author 32

Playing a sport, such as soccer, requires a lot of energy.

What Are Carbohydrates?

Maya and her teammates race down the soccer field. Her teammate has the ball. She passes to Maya. Maya kicks the ball toward the goal. She scores! By the end of the game, she is tired and hungry.

Strawberries and other fruits provide the body with carbs as well as other nutrients.

Maya's mother calls her over to the sidelines. Maya sits down by her mom and opens the cooler next to her. Inside are sliced strawberries and crackers layered with peanut butter.

"These snacks will help replace the energy you burned off playing soccer," her mom says. Eating them helps Maya feel ready to go home and start her homework. She likes feeling full of energy.

Important Nutrients

Carbohydrates (often called carbs) are **nutrients**. Nutrients are parts of food that people need to stay alive. Different nutrients help the body in different ways.

Carbs give the body energy. There are many forms of carbs. All fall into one of two categories. These categories are **complex** and simple.

Energy from Plants

People can get carbs from plants. Plants create a sugar called glucose, which they use for energy. Plants store chains of glucose. When people eat plants, their bodies break the chains into pieces. Then their bodies use the glucose for energy.

Carbs are found in many different foods that come from plants.

The difference between them is in how the body **digests** them. Complex carbs are digested slowly. That helps the body keep a steady flow of energy. Simple carbs are digested quickly.

They may give the body a quick burst of energy. But the energy does not last very long.

Carbs are in many foods. They are often found in food from plants. Grains, such as wheat and rice, have a lot of carbs. So do fruits, including bananas and strawberries. Dairy products, beans, peas, and some vegetables also have a lot of carbs.

Further Evidence

Look at the website below. Does it give any new evidence to support Chapter One?

What Are Carbohydrates?

abdocorelibrary.com/carbohydrates
-as-necessary-nutrients

Eating carbs gives people the energy needed for school and other activities.

CHAPTER 2

Why the Body Needs Carbs

Carbs give the body energy to live, work, and play. The body breaks carbs down into a sugar called glucose. The glucose then gives the body energy. The body can use the energy right away, or the body can put it in **reserve**.

Apples are high-fiber fruits.

Glucose that the body does not need either right away or in reserve turns into fat. The body may not react well if it does not get enough carbs. Too few carbs can cause someone to

be very tired. It can make someone feel weak
or dizzy.

Three Forms of Carbs

There are three forms of carbs: fiber, starch, and
sugar. Fiber is any part of plant foods that the
body cannot digest.

Storing Carbs

The body converts carbs into glucose.
What it doesn't need right away is
stored as glycogen in the muscles
and liver. The body uses this glycogen
when it needs more energy. The body
can store about 2,000 calories of
carbs. Calories are units of energy
people get from food. But when this
storage is full, the glycogen turns
into fat.

Pasta is a popular food that contains a lot of starch.

The fiber mostly passes through the body without breaking down the way other parts of the food do. Fiber helps people feel full longer. That way they might eat less and not feel hungry as quickly. Fiber also helps the digestion process. Foods that have fiber in them include vegetables, fruits, nuts, seeds, beans, and whole grains.

Starch is made up of sugars strung together. The body has to break them down in order to use them as energy. Foods with starch include bread, cereal, pasta, potatoes, peas, and corn.

Sugar is the most basic form of carbs. This is found naturally in some foods, like fruits, vegetables, and milk. Sugar is also added to foods, such as sweets and **processed** foods.

Simple and Complex

Carbs are either simple or complex. Simple carbs are sugars. They are found in soft drinks and sweets such as cookies, candy, and cake. Most simple carbs do not have other nutrients.

Cupcakes and other sweets contain simple carbs.

They are missing vitamins and minerals. Those nutrients are good for the body.

Complex carbs have those nutrients. The two types of complex carbs are fiber and starch. They are found in vegetables and whole-grain foods. Fruits contain both simple and complex carbs.

The body digests simple carbs quickly. This can give the body a quick jolt of energy. But it does not last as long as the energy that comes from complex carbs.

Explore Online

Visit the website below. Does it give any information about carbs that wasn't in Chapter Two?

Learning about Carbohydrates

abdocorelibrary.com/carbohydrates -as-necessary-nutrients

People who exercise a lot
need more carbs than
those who are less active.

Best Choices for Carbs

How many carbs each person needs to eat varies. It is not the same amount for everyone. It depends on the person's age, weight, health, and how active the person is. A doctor can help people learn what they need.

People can meet with nutrition experts, called dietitians, to get advice on how to plan healthy diets.

Dietitians, who are experts in nutrition, can also help. It is important to carefully choose the types of carbs to eat. While some simple carbs have valuable nutrients, many do not.

Cucumbers, tomatoes, and peppers are all good sources of fiber.

It is good to limit foods that have lots of added sugars. These foods have few nutrients. They do not provide long-lasting energy. They can also cause people to gain too much weight. People should always check food labels. They have details about what the foods contain.

Eating a balanced diet helps people get the right nutrients. A good way to do this is to eat from each food group every day. There are five food groups. They are fruits, vegetables, dairy, grains, and proteins. It is okay to eat foods with simple carbs sometimes too.

Look for Fiber

Foods that are high in fiber provide lots of energy. They also keep people full longer.

Eating Well

A balanced diet should contain foods from each food group. Foods with carbs are found in every group: fruits, vegetables, grains, proteins, and dairy.

Many fruits and vegetables are high in fiber. These include raspberries, bananas, broccoli, and carrots, among others. Another good source is whole grains. These are found in whole wheat bread, oatmeal, and brown rice.

Low-Carb Diets May Help Some People

Many people should keep carbs in their diets. But some people with medical concerns may benefit from eating fewer carbs. This includes people with epilepsy, diabetes, migraine headaches, and some cancers. People should ask their doctors to see if this diet could help them.

Most vegetables are packed with fiber. This helps people stay full after meals.

Refined grains have had some parts of the grains removed when they are processed. They are missing some healthy nutrients.

Nuts, which contain lots of nutrients and fiber, are great snack options.

Legumes, nuts, and seeds are good sources of fiber. Legumes are a type of vegetable. There are many to choose from. Black beans and kidney beans are legumes. Green peas and lentils are also legumes.

Carbs are an important part of a person's diet. They provide energy, fiber, and needed nutrients. Eating the right balance of carbs keeps the entire body healthy.

Primary Source

Experts at the Harvard T. H. Chan School of Public Health explain which carbs are best:

> The amount of carbohydrate in the diet—high or low—is less important than the type. . . . Whole wheat bread, rye, barley, and quinoa are better choices than highly refined white bread or French fries.

Source: "Carbohydrates." *Harvard T. H. Chan School of Public Health*, n.d., hsph.harvard.edu. Accessed 25 March 2022.

Comparing Texts

Think about the quote. Does it support the information in this chapter? Or does it give a different perspective? Explain how in a few sentences.

Nutrient Jobs

Carbohydrates provide energy to the body.

Carbs help the body digest food.

Carbs help
people feel full
after they eat.

The body can store
extra carbs to use when
energy is needed later.

Glossary

complex
made of multiple parts

digest
to break down foods and liquids so they can be absorbed

nutrients
substances needed for the body's health

processed
changed from its original form

refined grains
grains that have had nutrients removed when they
are processed

reserve
something stored away to use later

Online Resources

To learn more about carbohydrates as necessary nutrients, visit our free resource websites below.

Visit **abdocorelibrary.com** or scan this QR code for free Common Core resources for teachers and students, including vetted activities, multimedia, and booklinks, for deeper subject comprehension.

Visit **abdobooklinks.com** or scan this QR code for free additional online weblinks for further learning. These links are routinely monitored and updated to provide the most current information available.

Learn More

Golkar, Golriz. *The Digestive System*. Abdo, 2023.

Martin, Noelle. *Super Foods for Super Kids Cookbook*. Rockridge, 2020.

Index

complex carbs, 7–8, 15–17

energy, 6–9, 11, 13, 15, 17, 22, 26

fat, 12–13
fiber, 13–16, 22, 24, 26
food group, 22–23

glucose, 7, 11–13
glycogen, 13

nutrients, 7, 15–16, 20, 22, 25–26

plant, 7, 9, 13

simple carbs, 7–9, 15–17, 20, 22
starch, 13, 15–16
sugar, 7, 11–13, 15, 22

About the Author

Amy C. Rea grew up in northern Minnesota and now lives in a Minneapolis suburb with her family. She writes frequently about traveling around Minnesota and loves to spend time with her dog.